AF470245

A MINDFUL, DAILY POSITIVITY JOURNAL

Seek out something wonderful in every day and celebrate positivity by recording a memory or thought a day and create a year of happiness.

With a year of weekly spreads, punctuated with happiness and memory quotes, Wonderful Days can be used to jot down all the great things in your life . . . allowing you to, literally, count your blessings.

www.JournalsOfALifetime.com

NAME:

ADDRESS:

PHONE NUMBER:

EMAIL:

Wonderful Days
A MINDFUL, DAILY POSITIVITY JOURNAL

Week Starting :

MONDAY

TUESDAY

WEDNESDAY

THURSDAY

FRIDAY

SATURDAY

SUNDAY

ONE MORE

Week Starting :

MONDAY

TUESDAY

WEDNESDAY

THURSDAY

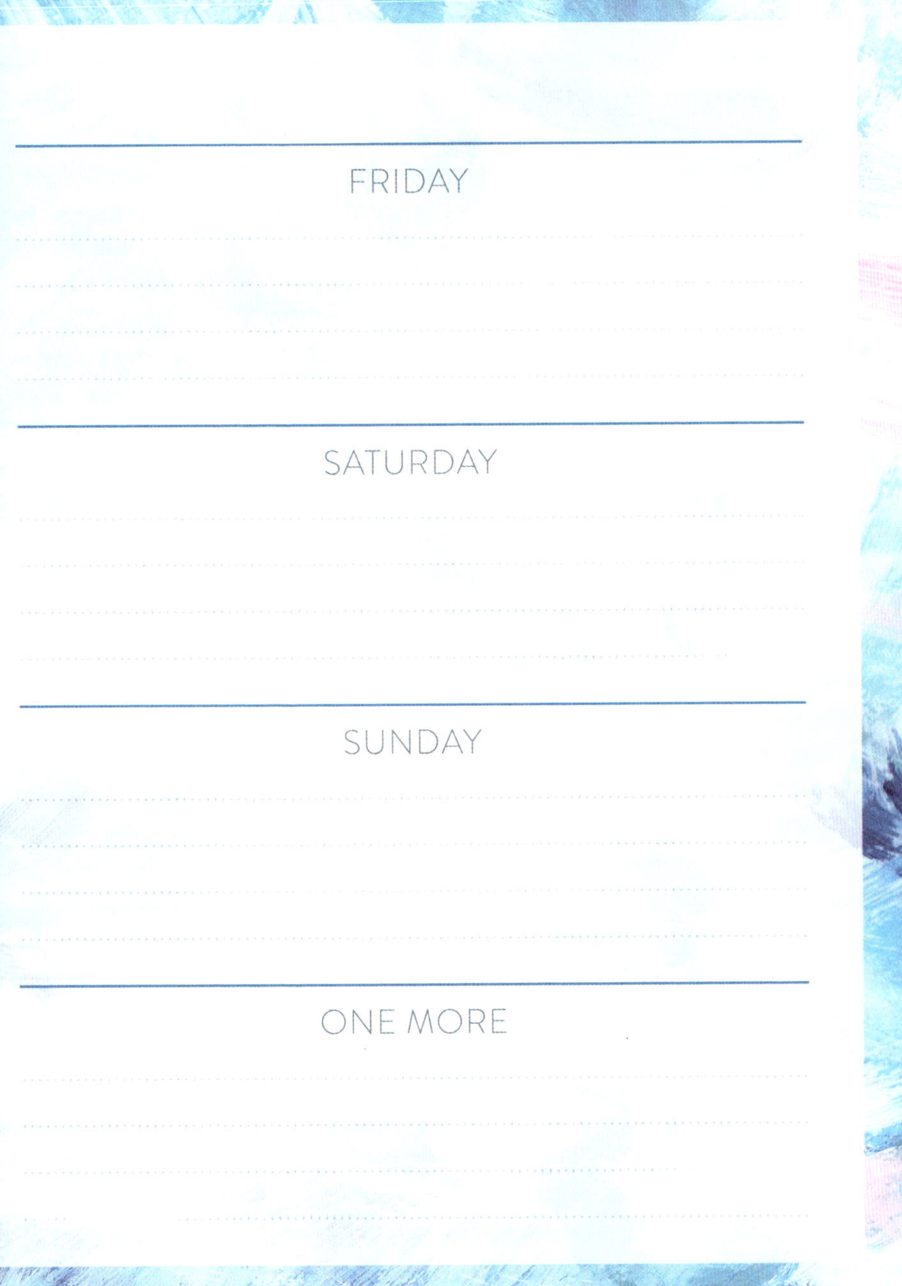

FRIDAY

SATURDAY

SUNDAY

ONE MORE

Week Starting :

MONDAY

TUESDAY

WEDNESDAY

THURSDAY

FRIDAY

SATURDAY

SUNDAY

ONE MORE

Week Starting :

MONDAY

TUESDAY

WEDNESDAY

THURSDAY

FRIDAY

SATURDAY

SUNDAY

ONE MORE

"Don't count the days, make the days count."
MUHAMMAD ALI

Week Starting :

MONDAY

TUESDAY

WEDNESDAY

THURSDAY

FRIDAY

SATURDAY

SUNDAY

ONE MORE

Week Starting:

MONDAY

TUESDAY

WEDNESDAY

THURSDAY

FRIDAY

SATURDAY

SUNDAY

ONE MORE

Week Starting :

MONDAY

TUESDAY

WEDNESDAY

THURSDAY

FRIDAY

SATURDAY

SUNDAY

ONE MORE

Week Starting :

MONDAY

TUESDAY

WEDNESDAY

THURSDAY

FRIDAY

SATURDAY

SUNDAY

ONE MORE

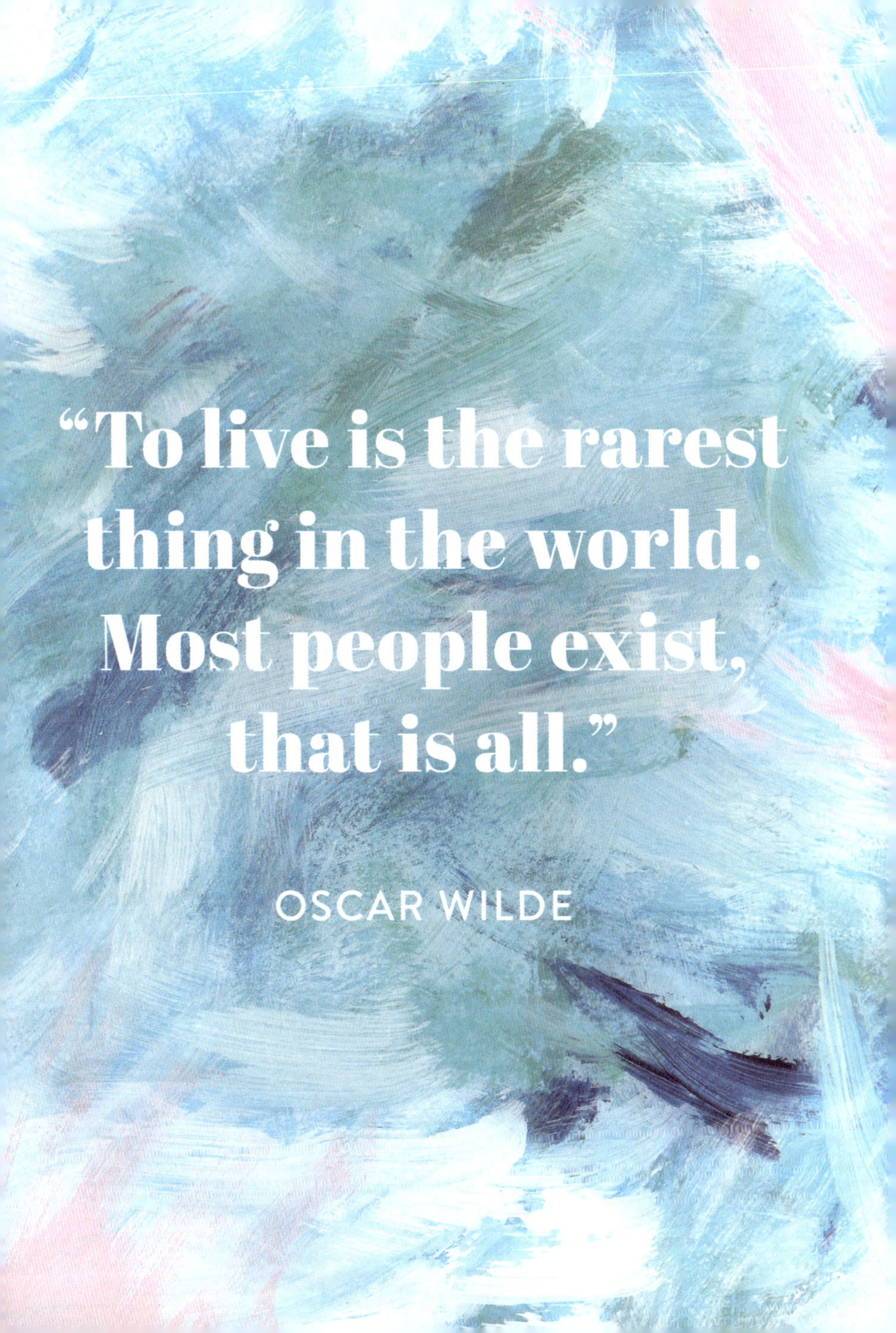
"To live is the rarest thing in the world. Most people exist, that is all."
OSCAR WILDE

Week Starting :

MONDAY

TUESDAY

WEDNESDAY

THURSDAY

FRIDAY

SATURDAY

SUNDAY

ONE MORE

Week Starting :

MONDAY

TUESDAY

WEDNESDAY

THURSDAY

FRIDAY

SATURDAY

SUNDAY

ONE MORE

Week Starting :

MONDAY

TUESDAY

WEDNESDAY

THURSDAY

FRIDAY

SATURDAY

SUNDAY

ONE MORE

Week Starting :

MONDAY

TUESDAY

WEDNESDAY

THURSDAY

FRIDAY

SATURDAY

SUNDAY

ONE MORE

"May you live every
day of your life."
JONATHAN SWIFT

Week Starting :

MONDAY

TUESDAY

WEDNESDAY

THURSDAY

FRIDAY

SATURDAY

SUNDAY

ONE MORE

Week Starting :

MONDAY

TUESDAY

WEDNESDAY

THURSDAY

FRIDAY

SATURDAY

SUNDAY

ONE MORE

Week Starting :

MONDAY

TUESDAY

WEDNESDAY

THURSDAY

FRIDAY

SATURDAY

SUNDAY

ONE MORE

Week Starting :

MONDAY

TUESDAY

WEDNESDAY

THURSDAY

FRIDAY

SATURDAY

SUNDAY

ONE MORE

"Wheresoever you go, go with all your heart."
CONFUCIUS

Week Starting:

MONDAY

TUESDAY

WEDNESDAY

THURSDAY

FRIDAY

SATURDAY

SUNDAY

ONE MORE

Week Starting :

MONDAY

TUESDAY

WEDNESDAY

THURSDAY

FRIDAY

SATURDAY

SUNDAY

ONE MORE

Week Starting :

MONDAY

TUESDAY

WEDNESDAY

THURSDAY

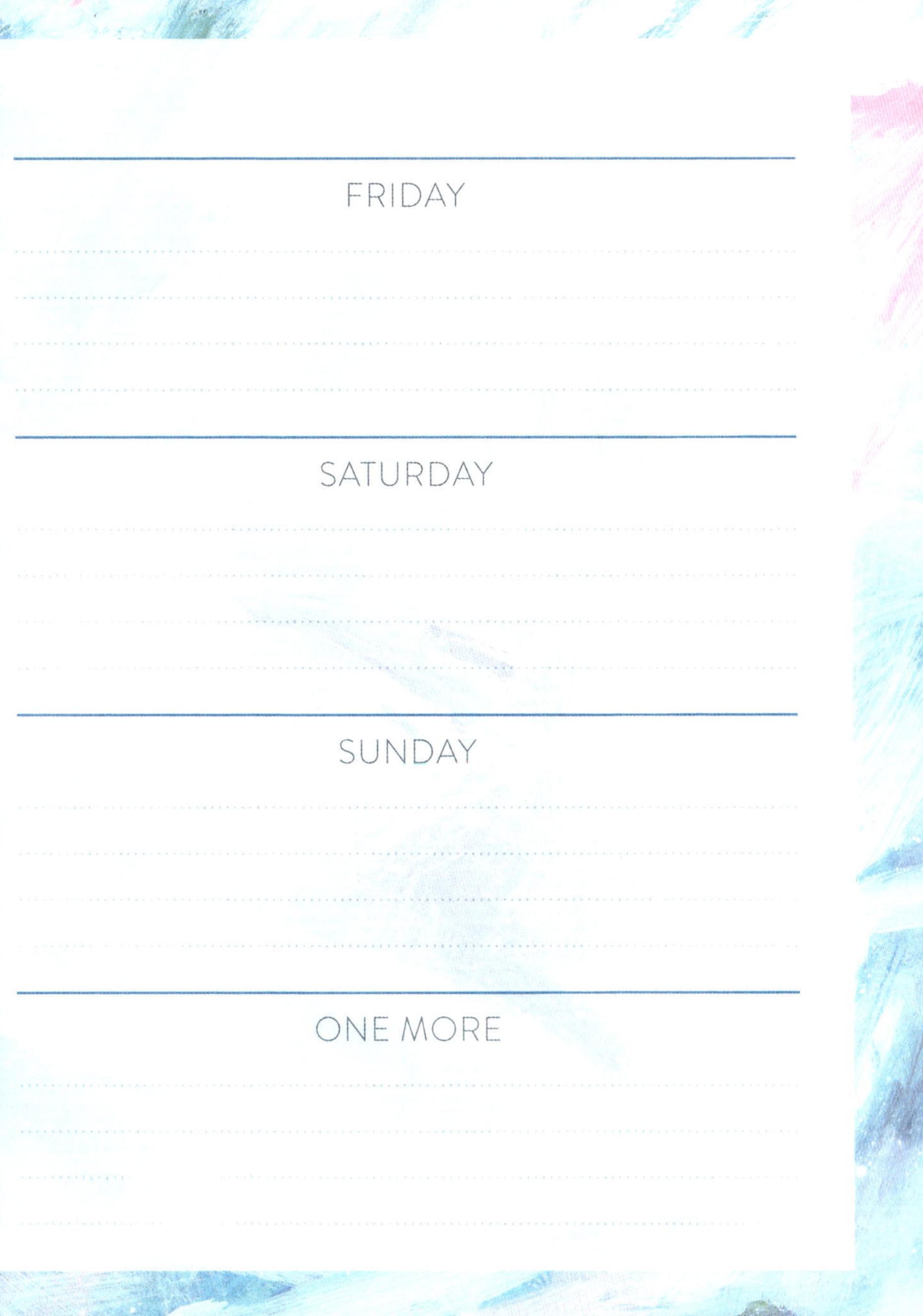

FRIDAY

SATURDAY

SUNDAY

ONE MORE

Week Starting :

MONDAY

TUESDAY

WEDNESDAY

THURSDAY

FRIDAY

SATURDAY

SUNDAY

ONE MORE

“There are always flowers for those who want to see them.”

HENRI MATISSE

Week Starting :

MONDAY

TUESDAY

WEDNESDAY

THURSDAY

FRIDAY

SATURDAY

SUNDAY

ONE MORE

Week Starting :

MONDAY

TUESDAY

WEDNESDAY

THURSDAY

FRIDAY

SATURDAY

SUNDAY

ONE MORE

Week Starting :

MONDAY

TUESDAY

WEDNESDAY

THURSDAY

FRIDAY

SATURDAY

SUNDAY

ONE MORE

Week Starting :

MONDAY

TUESDAY

WEDNESDAY

THURSDAY

FRIDAY

SATURDAY

SUNDAY

ONE MORE

"Start each day with a positive thought and a grateful heart."
ROY T. BENNETT

Week Starting :

MONDAY

TUESDAY

WEDNESDAY

THURSDAY

FRIDAY

SATURDAY

SUNDAY

ONE MORE

Week Starting :

MONDAY

TUESDAY

WEDNESDAY

THURSDAY

FRIDAY

SATURDAY

SUNDAY

ONE MORE

Week Starting :

MONDAY

TUESDAY

WEDNESDAY

THURSDAY

FRIDAY

SATURDAY

SUNDAY

ONE MORE

Week Starting :

MONDAY

TUESDAY

WEDNESDAY

THURSDAY

FRIDAY

SATURDAY

SUNDAY

ONE MORE

"Memories matter, pass them on."
NEIL COXON

Week Starting :

MONDAY

TUESDAY

WEDNESDAY

THURSDAY

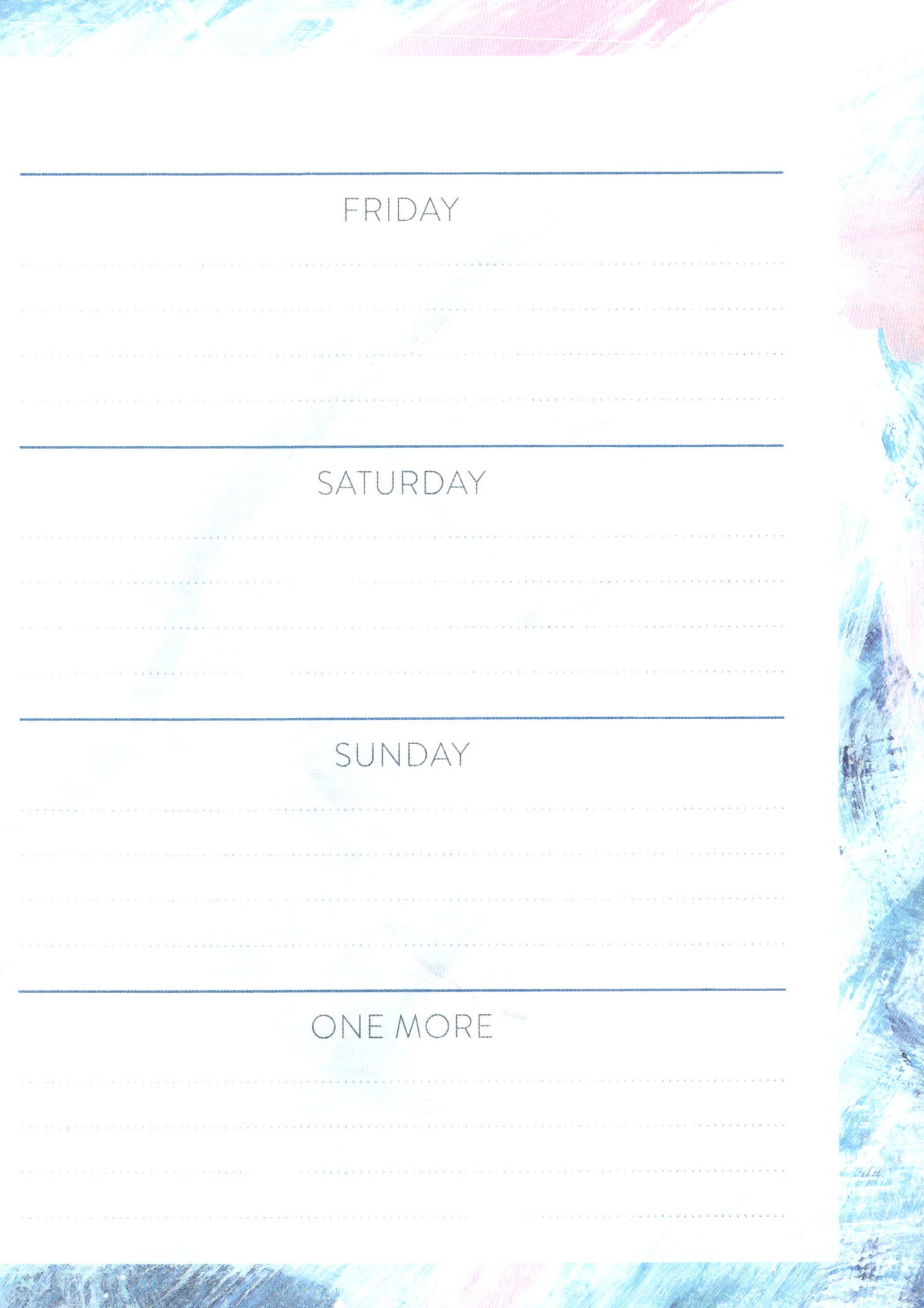

FRIDAY

SATURDAY

SUNDAY

ONE MORE

Week Starting :

MONDAY

TUESDAY

WEDNESDAY

THURSDAY

FRIDAY

SATURDAY

SUNDAY

ONE MORE

Week Starting :

MONDAY

TUESDAY

WEDNESDAY

THURSDAY

FRIDAY

SATURDAY

SUNDAY

ONE MORE

Week Starting :

MONDAY

TUESDAY

WEDNESDAY

THURSDAY

FRIDAY

SATURDAY

SUNDAY

ONE MORE

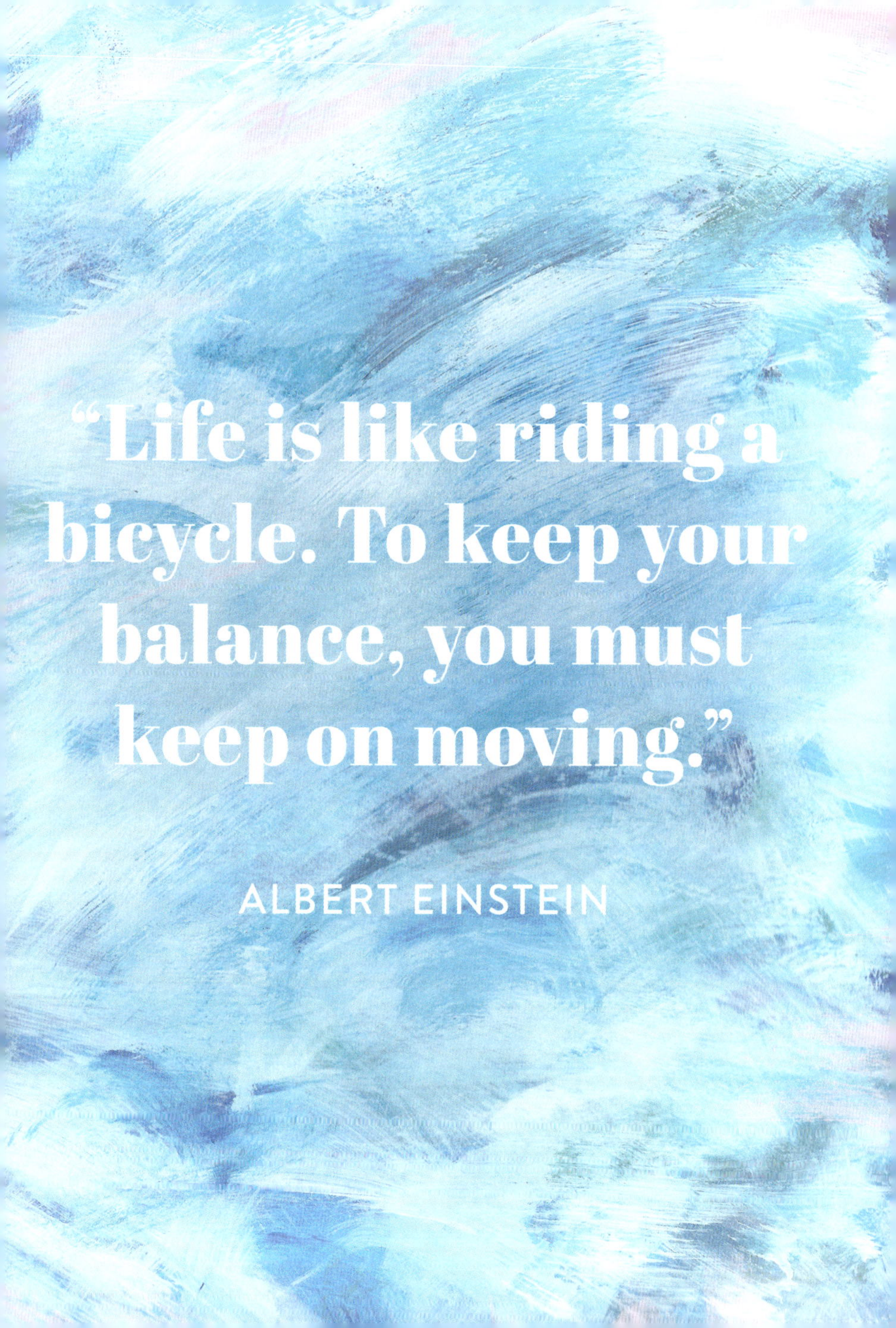
"Life is like riding a bicycle. To keep your balance, you must keep on moving."
ALBERT EINSTEIN

Week Starting :

MONDAY

TUESDAY

WEDNESDAY

THURSDAY

FRIDAY

SATURDAY

SUNDAY

ONE MORE

Week Starting :

MONDAY

TUESDAY

WEDNESDAY

THURSDAY

FRIDAY

SATURDAY

SUNDAY

ONE MORE

Week Starting :

MONDAY

TUESDAY

WEDNESDAY

THURSDAY

FRIDAY

SATURDAY

SUNDAY

ONE MORE

Week Starting :

MONDAY

TUESDAY

WEDNESDAY

THURSDAY

FRIDAY

SATURDAY

SUNDAY

ONE MORE

"Memory is a way of holding onto the things you love, the things you are, the things you never want to lose."

THE WONDER YEARS

Week Starting :

MONDAY

TUESDAY

WEDNESDAY

THURSDAY

FRIDAY

SATURDAY

SUNDAY

ONE MORE

Week Starting :

MONDAY

TUESDAY

WEDNESDAY

THURSDAY

FRIDAY

SATURDAY

SUNDAY

ONE MORE

Week Starting :

MONDAY

TUESDAY

WEDNESDAY

THURSDAY

FRIDAY

SATURDAY

SUNDAY

ONE MORE

Week Starting :

MONDAY

TUESDAY

WEDNESDAY

THURSDAY

FRIDAY

SATURDAY

SUNDAY

ONE MORE

"It's the possibility of having a dream come true that makes life interesting."
PAULO COELHO

Week Starting :

MONDAY

TUESDAY

WEDNESDAY

THURSDAY

FRIDAY

SATURDAY

SUNDAY

ONE MORE

Week Starting :

MONDAY

TUESDAY

WEDNESDAY

THURSDAY

FRIDAY

SATURDAY

SUNDAY

ONE MORE

Week Starting :

MONDAY

TUESDAY

WEDNESDAY

THURSDAY

FRIDAY

SATURDAY

SUNDAY

ONE MORE

Week Starting :

MONDAY

TUESDAY

WEDNESDAY

THURSDAY

FRIDAY

SATURDAY

SUNDAY

ONE MORE

"Nothing is ever really lost to us as long as we remember it."

L.M. MONTGOMERY

Week Starting :

MONDAY

TUESDAY

WEDNESDAY

THURSDAY

FRIDAY

SATURDAY

SUNDAY

ONE MORE

Week Starting :

MONDAY

TUESDAY

WEDNESDAY

THURSDAY

FRIDAY

SATURDAY

SUNDAY

ONE MORE

Week Starting :

MONDAY

TUESDAY

WEDNESDAY

THURSDAY

FRIDAY

SATURDAY

SUNDAY

ONE MORE

Week Starting :

MONDAY

TUESDAY

WEDNESDAY

THURSDAY

FRIDAY

SATURDAY

SUNDAY

ONE MORE

"Keep your face
to the sun and you
will never see the
shadows."
HELEN KELLER

Week Starting :

MONDAY

TUESDAY

WEDNESDAY

THURSDAY

FRIDAY

SATURDAY

SUNDAY

ONE MORE

Week Starting :

MONDAY

TUESDAY

WEDNESDAY

THURSDAY

FRIDAY

SATURDAY

SUNDAY

ONE MORE

Week Starting :

MONDAY

TUESDAY

WEDNESDAY

THURSDAY

FRIDAY

SATURDAY

SUNDAY

ONE MORE

Week Starting :

MONDAY

TUESDAY

WEDNESDAY

THURSDAY

FRIDAY

SATURDAY

SUNDAY

ONE MORE

"Every moment
is a fresh
beginning."
T.S. ELLIOT

Week Starting :

MONDAY

TUESDAY

WEDNESDAY

THURSDAY

FRIDAY

SATURDAY

SUNDAY

ONE MORE

Week Starting:

MONDAY

TUESDAY

WEDNESDAY

THURSDAY

FRIDAY

SATURDAY

SUNDAY

ONE MORE

Week Starting :

MONDAY

TUESDAY

WEDNESDAY

THURSDAY

FRIDAY

SATURDAY

SUNDAY

ONE MORE

Week Starting :

MONDAY

TUESDAY

WEDNESDAY

THURSDAY

FRIDAY

SATURDAY

SUNDAY

ONE MORE

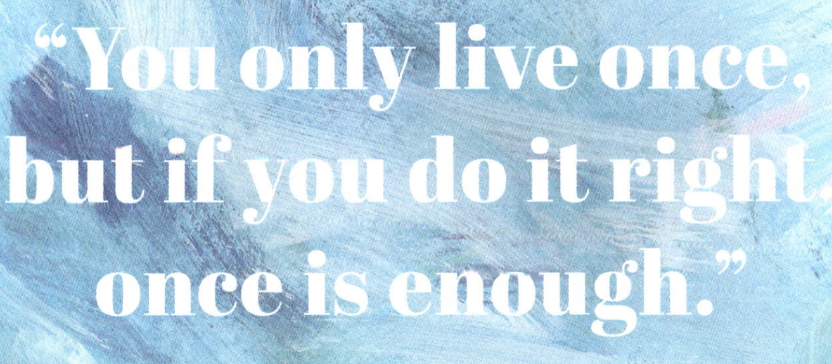

MAE WEST

Wonderful Days

A MINDFUL, DAILY POSITIVITY JOURNAL

The Mindful Collection, first published by Journals Of A Lifetime,
an imprint of from you to me ltd, in August 2018

www.JournalsOfALifetime.com

There are three titles in the collection:
Forward Thinking, This Is Me & Wonderful Days

To personalise journals and books as well as purchase
other products produced by us, please go to

www.JournalsOfALifetime.com

Printed and bound in China.
This paper is manufactured from pulp sourced from
forests that are legally and sustainably managed.

from you to me, The Old Brewery, Newtown, Bradford on Avon, BA15 1NF, UK

ISBN 978-1-907860-27-0

A JOURNAL OF A LIFETIME